# Welcome to
# Russia

by Alison Auch

Content and Reading Adviser: Mary Beth Fletcher, Ed.D.
Educational Consultant/Reading Specialist
The Carroll School, Lincoln, Massachusetts

Spyglass
BOOKS

COMPASS POINT BOOKS

Minneapolis, Minnesota

Compass Point Books
3722 West 50th Street, #115
Minneapolis, MN 55410

Visit Compass Point Books on the Internet at *www.compasspointbooks.com*
or e-mail your request to *custserv@compasspointbooks.com*

Photographs ©: Charles O'Rear/Corbis, cover; Keren Su/Corbis, cover (background);
Steve Raymer/Corbis, 4; Corel, 6, 7, 8, 12, 14, 15, 16, 17 (top); Peter Turnley/Corbis, 9, 13;
Svetlana Zhurkina, 10, 11; AFP/Corbis, 17 (bottom).

Project Manager: Rebecca Weber McEwen
Editor: Heidi Schoof
Photo Selectors: Rebecca Weber McEwen and Heidi Schoof
Designers: Jaime Martens and Les Tranby
Illustrator: Svetlana Zhurkina

**Library of Congress Cataloging-in-Publication Data**

Auch, Alison.
  Welcome to Russia / by Alison Auch.
     p. cm. — (Spyglass books)
Summary: Briefly introduces life in modern-day Russia.
Includes bibliographical references and index.
  ISBN 0-7565-0371-X (hardcover)
  1. Russia (Federation)—Juvenile literature. [1. Russia (Federation)]
I. Title. II. Series.
  DK510.23 .A83 2002
  947—dc21

# Contents

# Where Is Russia?

Welcome to my country!
I live in Russia.
I want to tell you about my
beautiful home.

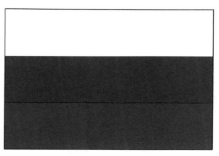

Russian Flag

## Did You Know?

Russia is so large, it has eleven *time zones.* The United States only has four.

ARCTIC OCEAN

RUSSIA

PACIFIC OCEAN

N
W E
S

0        1,000 miles

0     1,000 km

# At Home

I live in a big city called Moscow. My family has a nice apartment on a quiet street. Most people in Moscow live in apartments.

More than 1,000 people
live in each of these tall
apartment buildings!

# At Work

Everyone in my family works.

My mother is a doctor.

My father is a scientist.

My job is to do well in school.

# Beet Soup

In Russia, we eat a lot of bread, meat, and potatoes. I also like borsch. It is a red soup made from *beets.* I like it with sour cream.

On special days, we eat *traditional* foods and drink fruit juice.

# Warm Clothes

Moscow has warm summers and very cold winters. Russians have always known the best way to stay warm. They wear lots and lots of layers!

These women are wearing traditional Russian clothes. The bread and salt show *hospitality.*

# At the Park

In Moscow, we like to meet our friends at the park. When the weather is warm, we ride our bikes. When it is cold, we go sledding.

Gorki Park is very large. We can walk, swim, skate, and even play tennis there.

# Fun Facts

Most Russians take long vacations in the summer. They like to get out of the cities.

Russia is famous for the *domes* on the top of some of its buildings. These are called onion domes.

Russians love the arts. Many famous painters, writers, and musicians have come from Russia.

*Siberia* has the widest ranging temperatures in the world. In the summer, it can be almost 100° F (35° C). In the winter, it can be almost 95° below zero (-73° C).

# The Snow Maiden

Once upon a time,
there was an old
woman and man.
They were sad because
they had no children.

One winter day, they
made a daughter out
of snow. They loved her
very much.

When the warm summer came, the daughter was sad. She was afraid she would melt in the sun.

One day, she and her friends began dancing near a fire. When the daughter danced, she melted. Then she turned into a cloud and flew away.

# Glossary

**beet**–a red vegetable that grows beneath the ground

**dome**–something that is built in the shape of half of a ball

**hospitality**–actions that show that someone or something is welcome

**Siberia**–a very large area of land in the eastern part of Russia

**time zone**–an area of land that shares the same standard time. Each time zone is one hour different from the time zones next to it.

**traditional**–when people do something that has been done for many years

# Learn More

## Books

Harvey, Miles. *Look What Came From Russia.* New York: Franklin Watts, 1999.

Kendall, Russ. *Russian Girl: Life in an Old Russian Town.* New York: Scholastic, 1994.

Pluckrose, Henry. *Russia.* New York: Franklin Watts, 1999.

## Web Sites

www.ipl.org/youth/cquest

www.peacecorps.gov/kids/like/ russia-fun.html

# Index

**GR: F**
**Word Count: 224**

# From Alison Auch

Reading and writing are my favorite things to do. When I'm not reading or writing, I like to go to the mountains or play with my little girl, Chloe.